FABULOUS

Matthew Curry

GARVELLAN BOOKS

[1]

FABULOUS

First Published July 2020 by
Garvellan Books

FABULOUS

for Neil Bowen

Final Fable

There was a man read every fable
And absorbed every moral.
He was funny, wise, but unable
To do much else but quarrel.

Contents

Ode to Gaia

Whatever happens, you will be ok.
You don't require
Humans and the baggage they bring –
Powerstations, abattoirs, every bleeding thing,
Tarmac, pylons, housing,
Landfill, microplastic, kindling,
Coal, gas, electric fire.
Whatever happens you will be ok.

You don't need
People cluttering your planet, any more
Than you relied upon the dinosaur.
Maybe it would be a bore
If you never saw
Another boat, plane, car, tram, train, lawn mower,
I can't be sure
But I don't think your heart would bleed.

Whatever happens you will be just fine.
I don't think you'll pine
For fish farms, hydroponics, high rise flats,
Satellites, cheap flights, oil rigs, beer vats,
Automated milk maids, domesticated cats,
Palm oil plantations, dead infected bats.
Correct me if that's
Wrong, but I incline
To think whatever happens you'll be fine.

Perhaps you'll miss
Classical music – maybe Beethoven, Mozart.
Van Gogh, Picasso, Leonardo – great art,
The mind of a mathematician? Start

Collecting for your Desert Island Chart
If I were you, because it looks like this
Might be the last you see of us.
Get ready for loneliness.
I know, you'll miss us like a bad fart.
And whatever happens, it will be bliss.

U-Turn

I had a strange feeling the other day
That the Universe has turned around
And is heading the other way,

That is to say
Back from where it was bound
Towards some centre, far away.

Development

Past the estate of park homes I go
Some with tiled, some with old asphalt roofs.

Past the high hedgerows that will be cut through
To build on fields anew, anew.

Some protest placards have been put
Along the shady Shady Lane

People who've already got
A lovely house would really rather you

Didn't mess with nature's proofs
The way their builders did, again.

Cat

The neighbours' cat
Has been trying to get at the wrens.

I saw her in amongst the plants
Under the low eve where they nest.

Will she try to climb?
Or, more likely, is she

Waiting, an anticipant,
For when they try to fledge?

We do our best
To shoo her away each time

But I'm pretty sure we can't
Guarantee that when they start to fly,

Careering from gutter to hedge
We will always be there.

The chicks will have their test
And, when no one's looking,

[11]

With playful charm, I'll warrant,
The cat will use her knowledge.

Poppies

Last day or two
the big poppies,

just a few,
have thrown their

silk skirts on view.
Dramatic, flamenco,

with a fierce inner glow.
And the centre,

if you make yourself look,
it is as though

it wears no knickers,
and everything is on show.

Teasels

After the clematis flowers fade,
Where each bloom was
These other beings appear.

Silver, hairy, 'teasels'
My mother calls them.
They look like manufactured decorations.

Hard to believe that they have grown at all,
Are living, changing,
Provisional and frail.

Youth

Seeing kids walking along,
Mostly young lads
Heads back, gobs open,
Trying to catch warm summer rain

Takes me straight to those young years,
Those happily careless, aimless,
Yomping days I lived away
Lavishly, but would now prolong.

Salvia

The blue salvia by the back door,
The door that's ordinarily used
To come and go, to and from,

With ivy above and to one side.
The blue salvia stands, green in its big pot,
Holding aloft its two frail towers.

The Plot

So their sale has fallen through.
You get a lot of time wasters.
I daydream that I'll do
A book good enough, that masters

Form and fresh expression
So well, an avalanche of sales
Earns me, in short fashion,
Enough to tip their scales.

Charming

Mass is beamed into the kitchen
(Aga warmth, a sudden colder spell);
I pass through just as the antiphon,
I think it was, goes without response.
The atmosphere in there is calm, for once.
I'll go back shortly to make a brew,
Though the noise of the kettle won't go down well.
They don't do transubstantiation
Across the great mind of the internet, not yet,
But I bet it would work if they tried.
You may find this superstitious or blasphemous, but it's true,
A poem enacts the exact same kind of process, to wit:
Ordinary, found objects (words) are supplied
Which charmed change to a charm for changing you.

Honeysuckle and Thorn

She's wrapped around him
And it would seem

That she is more beautiful
While he is stronger.

But in their inner nature
(And here I must give you the dutiful

Truth), he is the sunbeam
She the muscled limb.

[15]

Honeysuckle and Thorn (2)

Little giveaway flecks
Of honeysuckle
There on a hawthorn
In the angled field.

She winds her sex
Around his tackle.
He stands forlorn,
Undone, revealed.

Beach Fires

We used to take the trailer up there
And scavenge wood for beach fires.
Those were the days. Eighteen, nineteen,
I would windsurf for five or six hours
Every day if the wind was good. Riding waves,
Tearing up and down the estuary,
Face catching salt sea spray, watching the patterns.
And then at weekends, a night fire on the beach.

How could we know then how time behaves?
And even had we known how could we care?
We were immune to world worry
And had our own immediate more important concerns
Like how to move to kiss, and hold, and reach
Bra clips and undo them before the moment expires.

Taller Than Herself

A leaf a stalk of grass a seedhead.
The girl holds her father's hand.
She must be about four and
In her other she holds
This long stalk of grass
Taller than she is
That he just picked for her over there.
Leaf, stalk, seedhead.
And she beams because she knows
Something very important
Has just been bestowed upon her.
She holds her head higher now
Meets any passing eye and grows
Taller than herself beside her father.

A Gift

The smoke bush, catinus,
Your sister-in-law bought
For your sixtieth

Which you brought North by train.
How that has grown!
Its dark red leaves, almost purple, earth

Your herbaceous border, stand at the back
Like a teacher in a school photo, caught
In a moment of quietus.

[17]

Ode to Rain

We hate you when you're here
But miss you
When you're gone too long.

This year
The lawn has been from lush to
Hard pan brittle yellow and back
Already.

As though a gong
Were struck
Earlier today

If I'm not wrong
About two o'clock
The clouds began to throw away
All they had become.

I thought I heard the garden sigh.
Remembering my youth
I stood outside like a bum

And head back let you fly
Into my mouth.
Yum yum.
I heard thunder

And watched lightning fork.
Made myself stand
In wonder.

Trickles talk

Down drainpipes. The land
Slowly goes under.
Becomes the brim.

My eyes are wet.
All my face.
Those are seraphim

Dancing in the clouds, I bet.
The waters race.
The day is getting dim.
Darkness is near.

Ode to the Fledgling Wrens

So you have all fledged
While the cat wasn't around.
Very wise. I thought you might have hedged

Your bets, gone one at a time
Over a number of days.
But no, like parachutists from a wartime
Plane, you tumbled out together in a daze.

You swooped and careered and landed
All over this green drop zone.
I kept my eye out as intended
Ready to throw a warning stone,

A piece of white gravel from the drive
If that brindled menace appeared.

[19]

But luckily she never did arrive,
And I watched your cute display with the coast cleared.

You would think the odds were stacked
Very heavily against you,
Observing how all obviously lacked
The necessary street cred. Who

Would ever gamble on you?
Why do I so root for you to survive?
Why do I hate that cat so?
She has an equal claim to be alive

And to do the things cats do.
Like me she is dependant
On a household round here. Like me too
She hunts a playful moment.

But the difference, I suppose, is that I'm
Trying to deliver a life
A new being when I toy with rhyme.
A kind of midwife.

Whereas she
Kills for fun
And doesn't even eat
When she's done.

So yes, hate is the word,
And I have taken sides.
I wish you well, my little wren birds.
My undercover guides.

Nails

I cut my toenails today
With my mother's curved little scissors.
They seem to be growing faster.
Or is it just that the days fray

And drag
And so time
Seems to lag

Behind my body's sense of the present?
Nails are keratin.
Am I right? A pleasant
Sense of the animal within,

Of growth
And death,
Both,

Is what clipping them gave me.
A sense that I am process.
A wave whose medium, matter, will be
Shed completely one day. I confess

I don't know
What then.
Who does though?

Perhaps another realm.
Perhaps not.
Can this wave I am overwhelm
Its physical lot?

Or just
Like a business
Go bust?

Or, as the bard said
Disencumber on the shore,
Its time all expired,
Its essence no more?

The Aga

When the Aga goes off in August
All the life seems to drain from the room.
It becomes a space like any other.

Normally a place of wonder,
Of baking, roasting, resting, of 'robust'
Argument. A hub, a kind of womb
Where family, extended family, dead family loom.

A place dominated by my mother.
Where love and hate and time are torn asunder,
Only to be reborn, again, again.

Except for that one month, when it just
Takes a breather, and all refrain.
And then the Aga returns, come September
When sideboards, table, walls, start to remember.

Colston

The tutor was 'well born'
If I remember right.
I had just given a paper on a thorn-
-y issue. I caught sight

Of Sanjida as I stopped,
And then the tutor looked at me and said:
'Yes, it's a bit of a n..... in the woodpile
That problem, isn't it.'

My eyes and Sanjida's met,
Fleetingly rolled, and we smiled.
I sank in my seat and let
My dreadlocks fall wild.

They were good dreads for a white.
Because, you see, my hair
Is very wiry, afro if you like.
Still, I was surprised he'd dare.

Why did I just sit there?
That's the moment, looking back,
I decided I didn't care.
And I never did wear a black

Gown. I suppose I was
In his eyes a provocation,
Just because
I was there. An irritation.

I remember him saying
Once, he didn't ever dream –

[23]

Perhaps his mind was fraying.
Things aren't always what they seem.

But perhaps all that is why
I felt a sudden, deep joy
To see that statue toppled by
Amongst others, a white, dreadlocked boy.

Mangey

Amongst the other local cats who prowl
There is a second brindled cat
From the same household.

A strange one this. Enigmatic.
But not in the usual catlike way.
Tiny. Timid, but insistent.

Powerfully so. As though it has been
Treated so badly
Nothing new really scares it.

Hoping for something.
Not looking to hunt at all.
Truly a heartbreaking sight.

In a dream of hunger.
One gluey eye. Too thin.
More than uncared for.

1st July 1987

I shouldn't have been there.
Pure luck to win a ticket
To Number One Court on the way down
In a coach I only got on at the last minute
Because my sister dragged me out of bed.
Becker was going for his third year
In a row, a hat-trick, a triple crown.
Already, aged nineteen, he seemed to own
The place. His strawberry blonde charisma, his physique, said
'Look on my works ye mighty, and despair'
Or might as well have. Tennis history strewn
In his extraordinary wake.
And then, enter Peter Doohan.
Dink after dink. Mistake after mistake ..

Sugar Slaves

Slaves and the sugar economy.
What is it with people?
The time value of money.

Cast iron clasps. We
Paid for the wonderful steeple!
With slaves and the sugar economy.

Investments. Ostensibly.
You know. What is it with these people?
The time value of money –

It's wonderful out there. Sunny.
Paid for this marvellous steeple!
The slaves! The sugar economy!

Molasses thick like honey.
We are the sugar people.
It's the time value of money.

This one thought it was funny
To run off. Strung up from a purple
Tree. Slaves, the sugar economy.

I even own her cunny.
And any kids these 'people'
Produce. These slaves. The sugar economy.
It's time. The time value. Of money.

Witch

I knew
An elder tree
That grew

In a wild place once.

Could it be
That what they say
Is true?

On the day
One is felled

A witch is set free?

She had been held
By tree and earth.
She yelled

Unheard
As the chainsaw cut.
Now the word

Is that that slut
Was summoned,
Who knows the worth

Of nothing.
Strange birth
It was that happened.

In a wild place once.

The Man With The Flag

1

The Towers Are Burning

Like two cigarettes jutting
From the mouth of America

The towers are burning

Cu-ckoo   Cu-ckoo

The back of the hills
Heather rough and lush

Cu-ckoo   Cu-ckoo

A single rowan tree
By the stream
Watches the world turn

Cu-ckoo

A single jet-trail across the sky

You lie in the darkness alone
Waiting for the right words to come
For the right strings of words to come

Waiting for things to reconfigure

Hanging on to the belief

That in reconfiguring words
The world is reconfigured

The towers are burning

2

The TVs Were On At Work All Round

So you were some of the first to see
And soon a crowd assembled in the shop

Afternoon in England
Watching in disbelief

Not knowing you were in the time
After the time before
But before the time after
After which nothing would be the same

Lives come and go like barley like grain
But something now will never be the same

3

A Little Stand Of Newly Planted Trees

Down by the river. The grasses high between.
Those green plastic collars. And then the deer
Against whom they are protection. Just here
The merest movement gives them to your eye.
Young and nervy, slowly passing by,
Heading upstream, upwind, unknowing.

[30]

The green leaves are all whispering,
The water whispers peaty dark and brown,
Your breath held momentarily on the breeze.

4

Both Planes In Their Elegance And Power

And in their utter destruction in each tower
And in the way each tower burned
And then collapsed one at a time
Under the burden of its own weight

The balletic way it happened was as much
And was as devastating
As what happened

The time before
And the time after

Cu-ckoo

5

Growing Frightened Of Yourself In Your Retreat

Waiting long enough to become patient
Waiting until it no longer feels like waiting

Only then the words
From their old stale fixed meanings
From their old stale fixed associations
From their old stale uses lose themselves

[31]

Only then the words renew themselves

Become
Once again
Themselves

6

A Man In A Tank Burned Back To A Grinning Skull

A conscript army fleeing back to Basra
The road to Basra strewn.

The time before
And the time after.

The oak stick the white oak stick swings
And stops and swings once more.

You catch it. Release it. It swings

7

The Girl Beside Me Wore A Jade Pendant

Or jadeite, less pure in colour
But richer.

Depicting a kylin. Carved.
What memory I am is turned to dust.
 I was on a hijacked plane.

You remember a path from long ago.
[32]

A path through your childhood.
Made of stone flags
Between high walls, descending.

Descending from a busy road
Straight down into countryside.
To a land of rusty barbed-wire fences
And conker trees.

And a pond in the woods
An old dark muddy pond
Under high, high trees.

A meadow with a horse and buttercups.
And then a further descent.
Down stone steps to a dirty river.

8

Napalm And Atom Bombs

Uranium-tipped shells.
White phosphor.

We thought we could do anything.
We thought we were unassailable.

The streets full of gawpers
Suddenly fleeing like frightened animals.
Choking on dust.

Some kind of sick confetti parade.

What? Did the Yankees win the world series again?!

Ticker-tape parade. We were joking around.
You're kidding me. What?
I was watching it. I saw it smash.

Two planes? Two planes.
Be advised we have jumpers.
A second plane hit.
The police want everybody off the road.
Reported fire on the 78th floor.

Did the Yankees win the world series again?

Some kind of sick confetti parade.

The towers are burning.

9

What Harm Is There In Sitting In A Tree?

In climbing trees?
Those lush floppy leaves all around.
The hard thin stems.

And earlier in the year
White candles still
Or nodding in the breeze.

10

It's Not Safe Here. It's Not Safe Here.

The firemen walk towards the towers.

[34]

Towards the burning towers.
Black with the yellow hi-viz trim.
The helmets with the distinctive broad rim.

I was watching it. I saw it smash.
Someone will pay for this.
These animals, they don't deserve to live on this earth.

This is the command post in tower two.
Oh he fell out. He fell out. The man with the flag.

Oh those poor people.

The smell is unbelievable.
The smell of burning wire.

Unbelievable.

11

A Cloudy Day But Dry

You sit on a boulder on the shore
With its hard dry tufts of lichen.

The estuary of the river Cree
Its surface ruffled by the wind.

The fast wingbeat of a snipe along the sea's edge.

The end of the day is coming.
The temperature is beginning to drop.
And as you think of going home
Of walking back up through trees

[35]

A patch of sea

A clump of sea

Is suddenly in sunlight
And the movement of light

Light on sea

Sea on light

A sudden shimmer that goes on and on
So that you can't tell the sunlight from the sea.

That movement implants
A sustained sense of intense uplift
That no painting or photograph or film can capture.
Complete rapture.

12

I Can Tell You That I Am Looking At Blue Sky

Where the South Tower once was.

It collapsed.
The top floors collapsed down.
I saw it go.
I just ran like hell.

The road to Basra strewn.

These animals, they don't deserve to live on this earth.

Oh my God.
Both towers down
Both towers.

Oh there's people hanging out the windows.
Oh he fell out, he fell out, the man with the flag.

Oh these poor people.

I just can't believe what I'm seeing.

The World Trade Centre is no more.

The time before.
And the time after.

It is Tuesday the eleventh of September
And you will not forget this day.

13

An Oar Over The Transom To Steer

Until there's water enough for the rudder to be lowered.

Ghosting out at first under jib alone.
Then the main and then the mizzen.
Now the rudder goes down and the oar is stowed.

The seawater slow in the zephyr.
Everything slow and serene.

The different coloured buoys of the moorings

The low tide rocks, their barnacles wet and looming.

We sit tight
Stealing a march on the tide.

14

And Then The Towers Came Down.

The barbarians are at the gate.

The towers are burning.

You flew low over the sea
Holding fast to the wishbone.

The waves were so powerful.
Neither benevolent nor malevolent .

And you harnessed and worked with their power.

The roaring sound of the waves when you're between them.

The constant change of their forms
Will not translate.

15

There Is The Time Before.

And the time after.
And that is all.
Lives come and go like barley, like grain.

[38]

Bodies strewn on the road to Basra.

Napalm and atom bombs.
The white heat.

Be advised we have jumpers.

The firemen walk towards the towers.

The time before.
And the time after.

Choreographed like a ballet.

The way they turned those planes.
Their long-haul fuel tanks full.

The graceful, sudden but graceful collapse.
All returning to dust.

I have no words.
I am empty.
I long to die.

To know forever
What is forever unknown.

I have no words.

Now I am ready to speak.

Rameses The Great

I have lain here for two thousand years.
The earth has kept me, my smooth features.
Once, I dominated a world. Once
Men prostrated themselves, were hurled hence.
Once. But you never know what might happen next.
Suddenly the world summoned a new text.
I fell, and broke, and lay in pieces
Here in the city of Heliopolis
Here under the slum of Matariyyah,
My smooth quartzite buried in a layer
Of soil and rubble and clay. My struggle
That seems like utter inertia. They keep me wet
Like some beached whale the humans might save yet.

A Breeze

This evening on the moor
A breeze came as from nowhere
Out of the hot still day
Out of the sunstruck land
Overlooking the azure sea
The crow-cawed tight-cropped fields
Yellow, with black bales of liquorice.

The breeze came as from nowhere,
The breeze came and kissed my skin
And with it came these words,
Brought by something unseen.

Mat

To see you on the mat once more
On your hands and knees, all your vertebrae
Visible, arched, concatenating, they ..
That is what I write this poem for ..
To be with you in that hot flat again
With no one known around us. Secretly.
The peopled block of others. Listening? Day
That may as well have been night. Grey
Walls like flesh but better.
Curtains closed above the modern square
Where schoolkids 'college' kids dropped litter,
Swarmed past on lunch break. Surely. Surely wore
Something of the urgency above.
The desperate rendings of our secret grave.

Heat

1

This heat is dragging my thoughts to you
A long time since our flesh last touched –
Your form is summoning me, or so
It seems, as though the hot heavy air clutched,
Drenched the distance, closed the gap, it is close –
Opening pores, drawing us from ourselves.
You must feel it, how the form of your face,
Your thighs naked above stockings, lace,
How your hair, trim there, how it delves
How a bead of sweat runs down your back

How I bite your earlobe bite your neck
You must feel it, I can feel your kiss,
Your delicate strength that will not stop until
You disappear like the wave's fizzing frill.

2

This oppressive heat is freeing me.
I no longer care, love more than ever,
Words run round all incidentally .
Your form unforms me, and the need to never
Go unguarded goes. Drops of sweat, the hum
Of fans moving on the burdened air
Moving on what stays on in this dumb
Body this dumb blood-beat drums up your
Voice your wrists your lips that move around my –
When did the windows the walls start to –
How does the ceiling – how do the books give off –
Whirr of your presence absence whirr of your shy –
Exact tilt of your nose the true
Location of my favourite mole, my love.

Barholm Woods

The road that passes through the woods
Runs up and round this little hill
From where the water-powered mill
Slowly sawed timber goods

For the estate. Now it's restored,
And tourists come and watch it turn,
And seeing nature harnessed, learn
An eco thing or two, or, bored,

Pretend to. I walk straight past,
And move up through the thundering sound
Of the wind in the woods. The ground
Is strewn with fallen trees from the last

Gales – this is just the after-blow,
When things seem fresh in their new places,
Each blade of grass each twig each fern have faces
That have passed a test. They know

Still-creaking slender oaks and pines,
With their ivy, with their insects, with their moss,
They know that mother nature is their boss,
And that deep, deep below us, she reclines.

The Divorce

1

It was as if the Anglo-Saxon
In us said, collectively, 'Enough!'
As though King Harold never lost his eye
And the Normans had retreated from the fray –
Vikings really, bully boys, just tough
When they're on top. But in this sour season –
It was as if the Norman churches, Norman keeps
Never came to dominate our land
Never turned the 'English' to Ireland
Never made the sore that weeps and weeps.
That moment, the North was never 'harried'
And Scotland wasn't dominated down
And Wales was not subjected to the Crown –
But then truth slowly dawned – and carried.

2

Don't duck responsibility.
There is no pure and pristine state.
Diversity's our vivid vibrant fate.
We're all our influences, we
Sang difference throughout history.
We sung this whole world into being
Not with blinkers on, not with seeing
Only what it's comfortable to see.
A child of mine taught English to his friend,
Whose family had left a world behind,
Whose family had high regard for England.
What can I tell them now, what can I say,

That we who had been open turned away?
When power fled, we fled to fantasy?

Sea Mist (2)

The sea mist is suddenly here again;
Closing down thought, closing down vision.
Is the shore really no longer there?
Are there trees at the end of the field?
Where

The red kite hangs in the, hangs in the air –
Or can it any longer? Or can it?
Does the water of the sea remain?
How take bearings without an horizon?

My room is full of sea mist now. My room!
I can't write; only try to remember this;
That this is the, this is the self-same;

Covering the sea, covering my eyes,
Filling my lungs, condensing, drowning.
What

Is the how is my mind where am I?

For A Friend Who Was Dying

I sit in the mazy heat. The fans turn
Their blurring circles above my head.
All the books scream for my attention.
How can it be that we will all be dead –
The sweet taste of blood in my mouth
The page blurring and the pen a blurr –
Christ every, everything is heading South.
Even the kids bright and eager as flowers,
The years spin away towards the end,
Fifty, forty more if we're lucky.
But you, my so composed friend,
Not so many months for you now. Sucky sucky
On time's lollipop. Now it's a hurry.
We'll all be with you soon enough. Don't worry.

Upon Westminster Bridge

It is afternoon, and the Thames glides by.
The Sweet Thames, the patient, the put-upon.
Sirens and cameras and people urgently
Getting away from danger. Bodies strewn ..
And helicopter blades, security ..
A strange garment now this city wears:
Swirling frantic noise, swirling lights,
The London Eye stock still above the sights.
Whisk me away from this strange city,
Whisk me away from all the Earth's cares.
Oh Thames, take me back to Fallujah,
Coax me downstream past the Isle of Dogs
Take me via Mosul, Baghdad, let me see the
Thousands upon thousands there in body bags.

Fabulous

Thirty-Four

New Versions of Old Fables

Often Attributed to Aesop

The Lion and the Mouse

When the mouse woke the lion
The lion got cross
And was just about to toss
The little creature to his death when Brian,

For that was the name of the little mouse,
Said 'I would be such an unworthy prey
For so great a hunter as you. What say
You let me go back to my tiny house.

'I'm sorry that I woke you
And one day, you never know
Maybe I will help you.' 'So
You, my little itsy-bitsy cook-a choo,

'You think that I, the great king
Of the jungle might need you?
Now that is funny' And he started to
Laugh. He laughed and laughed. 'Sling

Your hook, go on, and don't Ever ..'
'I won't, don't worry, your Majesty
Your Eminence, your ..' and he beat his hasty
Retreat. Years later, however,

A strange thing happened.
The mouse was out wandering along
When he heard a strangled roar, a sad song.
He followed the trail of the sound.

And do you know what he found?
The lion caught in hunters' nets,

The self-same lion. A mouse never forgets.
He tiptoed across the danger ground.

The lion was hopelessly tangled.
It took a while before
The lion even saw
The mouse. This new-fangled

 Trap was so secure. But the lion recognised
Him then. 'Hello Mr Lion Sir,
We'll soon get you out of there'
And Brian began to gnaw. Despised

And disregarded most of the time
The little mouse, now an essential worker
Saved the day, saved the blonde berserker
Wrapped up in the nets. But hold the rhyme:

Imagine if the lion had killed the mouse
At the beginning of our story.
Why then the lion would meet a gory
End, and live on only as a rug in a grand house.

The Grasshopper and the Ant

The grasshopper sang all summer long
He gave and he gave and he gave.
Like it or not he transmitted his song.

The ant, who was afraid of the grave
Worked hard all summer gathering food.

She worked like a, worked like a slave.

(And look, I don't mean to be rude
But it wasn't food that she had made
It wasn't food that she had grown. But I'll intrude

No more). Come winter, in her quiet glade
The ant was settling down to dinner
When guess who should invade

Her privacy and quiet? That sinner,
That lazy, improvident grasshopper.
The ant had never seen him thinner.

He begged for food, this interloper.
'You should have thought of this back in the summer'
Said the ant to the no-hoper

'I know, life can be a bummer
If you don't plan in advance.
I worked all fucking summer

So I tell you what. Dance!
Dance the winter woes away!'
And didn't give him another glance.

The grasshopper didn't know what to say
So he left, humiliated.
And he sang a sad song. To this day

You can hear it. Under-rated.
He sang a famine song. Next year
He returned, a different insect. Waited

Down at the beautiful glade, where

The ant had lived. The place was changed.
No sign of the ant there.

Eventually, a young ant, looking deranged
Arrived. 'Who are you?', he asked.
'I'm a friend of the ant, well, .. estranged.'

'She's dead. My mother. Crops failed.' It unmasked
The boy's grief to say it, and he cried.
'Sorry for your trouble. I had uncasked

Something rather fine to share.' 'She died ..
When she, just before she died, she mentioned you. "Apologise
To the grasshopper for me, would you," she said,

"I thought he was a fool, but he was wise.
He knew the value of his song".'
'Ah, thank you', said the grasshopper, and went along.

The Crow and the Pitcher

First of all, the thirsty crow
Tried to push the pitcher over, like so.

It wouldn't budge. He had a think.
You see he really really wanted a drink.

How in the name of bleedin' heck
Can I get to the water below the neck?

He walked around – you know how they strut!

The problem really was doing his nut.

He flew to the nearest tree, and then
Guess what, he flew straight back again.

Up in the tree he'd had an idea.
Rushed back quick because of the fear

That he'd forget his clever fix
Which was to drop a load of sticks ..

No, stones is better, on second thoughts
They'll drop to the bottom and .. the level ought ..

Let's try it and see, the voice in his head
Told him. So that's what he did.

The Ape and the Fox

After the lion eventually died
The animals needed to choose a new king.
They met in a broad clearing
As long as it was wide.

Nobody really knows why the ape
Was chosen, but everyone agrees
That he was, even his fleas.
He wasn't the brightest, but he was in good shape.

His reign didn't last more than a day.
The crafty fox was jealous you see

[55]

And told him he'd found a delicacy
That he'd enjoy, in the woods, and led him away.

The ape really wasn't the brightest chap
He was greedy, and the crown
Went straight to his head. What a clown!
And the fox had set this baited trap.

Well the ape just walked right in
And no sooner had he got his mits
On the gorgeous basket of titbits
Than the trap was sprung. No use fightin'.

The fox invited all the animals to look
And once they were gathered he said:
'He wants to rule us. He can't rule his own head!'
And he laughed so hard his brush shook.

What happened next, I wonder?
Nobody knows, I'm afraid.
Myself I think they made
The ape abdicate, tore the crown asunder.

The Dog and its Reflection

There was this dog looking very pleased with himself
But also a bit secretive. There was a reason.
He had in his mouth a large steak he had just stolen
From the butchers. On the edge of the counter shelf.

Almost the whole town had gone after

The wicked dog, but he was too fast
Knew the terrain too well, and soon enough lost
Them. If his gob wasn't full you'd have heard laughter.

As it was, there was just drool
Dripping from his salivating mouth
And fire in his eyes. Heading South
Before too long he encountered 'the pool'

Which was really just a slow wide part
Of the river. He knew that once he'd crossed
They'd never have a chance of catching, he'd be lost
And could find a quiet spot to start

To eat. So in he went, swimming
In the style that dogs call 'human learner'.
The waters were smooth. Beer from a taverner
It could have been. Brimming.

Suddenly, the dog saw another
Dog in the water carrying
What looked like a better, bigger piece of meat. Dropping
His own, he grabbed at the other

Which was only his reflection after all.
The juicy steak was lost, drifting unseen
In the darkest depths of the river's dark spleen.
The dog made for the far bank, feeling small.

The Bald Man and the Fly

A mosquito bites a bald man.
Why is that funny?
Shouldn't we rather show concern?!

After all, malaria, dengue, many
Awful diseases are spread this way.
But a slap-head with a spot, for my money

Is one of the more amusing things in life. Stay
With me, because he's about to make it worse:
The bald man slaps the spot, attempting to slay

The cruel beast. But the fly has moved first.
'You'll only hurt yourself even more
Retaliating like that. Do your worst,

Man without even one hair.
You look ridiculous. Not a follicle!
Slapping your own head in mid air!'

'Why, you evil little disease-spreading diabolical
Wretch! I'll slap and I'll slap and I'll slap
If only I can destroy your every last molecule!'

In this way the tiny mosquito tortured the big bald chap.

The Fox and the Grapes

There was this old grey fox
And he was hungry.
And he saw these luscious young grapes
Just hanging from a vine.
They were hanging high.
Still in their bobbysocks.
His brush went 'swish'. They're mine!

With all the spring
In his hind legs
He jumps!
But even the lowest bunch escapes
His lunge. He thumps
Back down to the ground. He jumps
And he jumps. But no. 'Thing

Is', he says, as though
Anyone is listening.
'Things is' he says, with such
Authority as he can muster:
'Those grapes aren't ripe. Much
Better left. I don't need sour grapes.'
But no one believes his bluster.

The Farmer and his Sons

This is a sad one. A farmer calls his sons
And tells them, in confidence

Not to divide the family land,
Because hidden on it somewhere, there's treasure to be found.

Not to divide it when he dies he means.
And he is dying, that's why the scene's

Sombre and serious. Very much so.
They're worried about Pa of course. Though

The first thing they do is go straight out and dig.
They dig the whole farm over. And it's big.

Though not big enough to make three separate farms.
They find nothing. Their father dies in their mother's arms.

Next season, however, there is a bumper crop,
And the boys understand their father's wisdom. Stop.

The Farmer and the Sea

A farmer saw a ship get wrecked
He watched it all from the shore.
The sea had kicked up quickly and
The sailors all went to the sea floor.

But it didn't happen quickly
It was a long drawn out affair
The ship got caught on a savage rock
The one out, just over there.

The farmer watched and witnessed
Desperation as the waves
Huge and fizzing and powerful
Smashed them to their graves.

'What have you done, Thalassa,
Great Goddess of the Sea?
Why have you taken all these men
So needlessly?'

The Goddess rose from the ocean
Rose up high as a hill
And with a silky booming voice
Addressed the farmer, Phil:

'Nothing to do with me old boy
It's the winds that blow the sea.
Otherwise I'm as gentle as
Your orchards, your sweet soft lea.'

Death and the Woodsman

An old woodsman had journeyed a long, long way
Carrying an outrageously large bundle of heavy sticks.
In fact his whole life, every working day

He had either been cutting or carrying. Suddenly six
Hours into this day and six before its end
Something deep inside him broke. Like sticks.

You know, not whippy sappy ones that bend,
Things so dry and hard and old and brittle
That they snap. That was how it was. Friend,

It was an awful sight to see. A proud man's mettle
Gone. A broken man. Three score years and ten.
As the kids these days would say 'Lost his bottle.'

So he just lay down inside the glen,
Eyes up at the blue corridor of sky
And called on Death to deliver him of life's burden.

Straightways Death saunters up, all friendly.
With a 'Was there something you were wanting there wee fella?
You're not so happy down here evidently.'

Seeing Death, his smoothness, his umbrella,
The old man suddenly flinched and changed his tune
'I, I just called out for help, my burden fell, a

Little lift, and I can get delivered soon.'
'Oh you can get "delivered" all right', said Death,
'Any time you like. You see that Moon?

'Wherever you see it, remember, your last breath,
You come to me. In the meantime, here,
Let's get you up and running on the path.'

'Thank You, Sir', said the woodsman. Fear
Had put some life into the old boy,
And he stepped off almost lightly, almost with joy.

The Bulls, the Lion, and the Fox

It's the old story, divide and conquer.
A marvellously maned lion
Anywhere, anybody's champion,
Had his eyes on that field over there.

Four bulls grazed in it. All four,
He knew, would be too much
For even he to overcome. 'I'm strong, but such
A fight would not end in my favour.'

He was a brave but realistic beast.
So he employed the services of fox,
To sow enmity and discord among the ox-
-en. 'That way I can kill and feast

Upon them, one at a time'
He confided to his red-haired friend.
The fox did well, and by the end
Some choice cuts came his way. End of rhyme.

The Ass and the Pig

The ass in the barn watched as each day
A prize pig was fattened up on all he could eat
Of barley. 'He doesn't work like me'

The ass thought. 'I don't get such fayre.'
And over time became resentful.
Eventually, once the farmer was satisfied,

There came a day the pig was turned to meat.
The farmer slit his throat, filled jugs-full
Of his blood, whose wet sweet smell filled the air.

Next day the ass found he was supplied
With the self-same barley the pig had had.
The leftover. What remained. The ass

Wouldn't touch the grain. 'Bad
Vibes man', is how he explained his choice,
And 'You saw what happened to the pig, how he died ..'

The Raven and the Snake

The raven was ravenous
(Do you like what I did there?)
None of your usual superfluous
Barrel rolls in the air.

This time it's serious.
He has been scouring the harsh country
Seized by drought. He is getting delirious.
Dry, the land is. Yellow grass. A sad sentry

He looks, yon raven. He decided to give
It one more go today. His dry feathers
Lifted him graciously up. 'Not long to live
With no food in these new hot weathers'

He thought. Just then, as he glided
His cool shadow across the hillside,
Just before he decided
To pack it in, guess what he spied?

A black snake basking in the late sun.
Coiled, motionless, probably asleep.
And in his hungry opinion
It was at least worth a peep.

So back he soared, closer, and slowed
As he approached the big flat rock
Whose sun-warmth almost glowed.
The snake looked like the dial on a sun clock.

The raven cast his cool shadow
Long across the snake, who was, indeed, asleep –

[65]

Without thinking, the bird swept low
Swooped and seized the snake. Weep

For what happens next. The raven thinks
He has been unbelievably lucky. This solves
Everything. But he snake wakes and sinks
Her poison fangs into the bird, who dissolves

In pain, quickly loses height
And lands, down in the valley.
The snake only has to wait. She judged it right.
And soon the raven's jammed inside her belly.

The Eagle and the Fox

The eagle and the fox were firm friends.
You can already guess where this ends ...

Anyway, the eagle had hungry chicks.
And the fox had cute little cubs. Something clicks

Inside the eagle one day. I think it was a Monday.
He seizes the fox's cubs and flies away

Up to his eyrie in the top of a tall pine
(The view from which, by the way, was simply divine.)

And feeds their mangled bodies to his brood.
The ugly half-blind chicks don't recognise their food.

Bits of red fur drift softly on the air,

One lands on the fox searching for his cubs there.

He has been going crazy all day long,
Missing their yapping, play-fighting throng.

The truth hits him like a thunderbolt.
The eagle's had them. It's all my fault

For befriending such a high ranking one as he
Thinking even for a moment one so powerful would be ...

Fox still has his wits though in his grief,
And sets about his vengeance. I'll be brief.

He gathers sticks and twigs, tinder dry.
Stacks them round the pine, and then goes by

A human temple. He picks out a burning stick
From the sacrificial altar. Quick,

Quick he runs back to the pine tree,
Lights the pyre, and watches closely.

(The altar was consecrated to the Fates,
Who saw all.) The fire accelerates.

The eagle is away and won't return
Until the conflagration's ceased to burn.

The fat chicks quickly fry and, cooked, fall
To the foot of the tree. The fox devours them all.

The Fox and the Crow

The clever crow has found a piece of cheese.
I won't tell you where though.
She flies heavily under its weight, she's
Unconsolably happy with herself you know.

Thing is, she's single, and a little bit, well,
Between you and me, her self-esteem ..
Anyway she starts to eat. The smell
Attracts the dapper Mr Fox. 'Do I dream?'

He addresses the bird. 'Can this be real?'
He goes on. 'Such beauty I have never seen!
Glory! Hallelujah! Please, would you reveal
If your voice has also this marvellous sheen?'

The crow has swung straight from happy to flustered.
Deeply flattered though. Blushing under her black.
'Stunned by your beauty, I only just mustered
The courage to even speak', the fox pushes his attack.

'Well, I, thank you very much' the crow caws
In her scratchy voice. The cheese drops
Down from the tree where she's perched. The fox's jaws
Have it now. And off he pops.

The Rivers and the Sea

One day the rivers said to the sea:
'Our sweet waters are tainted by thee.
Everyone agrees you make them so salty
No one can drink it ever again, see.'

The sea was deeply unperturbed by this.
She drew herself up proudly, and said: 'Sis-
-ters, Sisters please. If you don't like my bliss,
Don't make contact with me any more. Don't kiss.'

The Donkey and the Icon

'Everywhere I go , lately'
Said the donkey,
To whom a religious icon
Had been strapped, to parade
Around with, some time before.

'Everywhere I go these days, the crowds adore.
It's no charade
I am their one!
Their Mr Funky!'
He said, intently.

The Wolf and the Heron

You know what wolves are like.
Your parents told you 'Don't wolf your food!'
Well, this wolf had been eating a pike.

Don't ask where he got that from dude.
About half way through, a sharp, fine bone
Lodged in his throat. Like it was superglued.

Like a branch jammed under a river bridge. Moan?
The dude was in such pain he howled,
But quietly, so's not to move the bone.

Ah man he must've been in pain. Scowled
And coughed, eyes out on stalks. The works.
He wheezingly begged the animals for help. Only the auld

Heron, he of the long bill, agreed. The other jerks
Didn't believe the wolf when he promised the earth.
'There will be a fantastic reward'. But the idea of perks

Paled beside the risk. It wasn't worth
The trouble. So the heron it was put his head
After his bill, down into the old wolf's mouth.

Like a surgeon's tweezers his beak caught and lifted
The bone, out from the pained wolf's throat.
'Now', said the heron, 'What will I be gifted?'

'Oh no no no you've had your prize, you old goat'
Said the wolf to the heron. 'Your head inside a wolf's gizzard
And lived to tell the tale, you old lizard.'

[70]

The Tortoise and the Hare

You'll know the story.
But what you might not know
Is how the hare
Ridiculed the tortoise.

'Mr Slow Coach
You're so slow
The humans only mention you
In an idiom for going to the loo:

'"The turtle is poking its head out"'
'Oh no no no' said the tortoise
I'm a tortoise not a turtle.
That's like confusing a dolphin
With a porpoise.'

'So you're so sloooow
You're known for nothing?
Not even for poking your head?'

'I get where I want to get
By the time I want to get there.
Some whizz around all over the place
But never get anywhere they want to go
Because they don't know.'

The tortoise let this pointed reply
Have the time it needed to cut deep.
But the hare wasn't even aware
That the tortoise meant him.
He was pretty dim.

[71]

'Well if you're so clever
At getting from A to B
Why not have a race with me?'
Said the hare,
Hoping to humiliate the tortoise.
Assuming he would decline.

'Yes sure. Fine' said the tortoise
'One hundred miles. No water', he added.
'Whatever', said the hare.

Word got out about the race.
Everyone's iphones were out.
From Athens to wherever it was, and back.

Predictably enough the hare went off
At breakneck speed,
While the tortoise took it slow and steady
In the hard heat.

After an hour or so the hare
Could hardly fill his lungs with air,
Had sweated lots of moisture out
And needed to stop for a break.
He fell asleep in some shade.
Big mistake.

The tortoise sauntered on
Enjoying scenery that was new,
Listening to the different sounds
Of new places.

Without knowing it he passed the hare
Somewhere in the wayside there.
But still he was far from done.

[72]

About an hour later the hare awoke.
The local badger, a decent bloke,
Told him the tortoise had passed long since.
That made the hare wince.
And off he went.
But he was still half asleep you see
And he headed off the wrong way.

It took him a while to notice his mistake.
He was so fast he's gone almost half way back.
He turned. He was getting tired now.
But eventually he caught
The tortoise, or so he thought.
By then, the tortoise was on his way home.

So the hare sped past
With an impending vast
Sense of panic and doom
His heart going boom boom boom
His lungs burning burning
His legs going jilly jolly jelly.
The tortoise smiled.

The hare reached the halfway point and turned.
But not like those graceful swimmers do,
All poise and flow. Oh no.
He was the opposite of that.
He never stopped trying though.
I have to take my hat off to that.

Halfway back from halfway though,
He needed to rest once more.
Actually he felled to the floor.
Collapsed. Splat.
Fatigue and dehydration can do that.

[73]

Meanwhile, the tortoise was almost home.
The animals lined the streets.
YouTube, Twitter, Tik Tok, and Instagram
Gave him fifteen minutes of fame.

'Will they never learn?' the tortoise thought
As he watched them running around, caught
In the constant fear of missing out.
'Has this lesson taught them nought?'

So he won the race
But waited with grace
For the hare to appear.
And when he did he didn't mock,
He put an arm round the exhausted shoulder:
'"Festina lente", "hasten slowly", the Latins say', he said,
'You'll learn the wisdom of that as you get older.'

The Crab and the Fox

A cab crawled from the sea shore
To seek his fortune in a field.
Whereupon the fox revealed
The meat inside its claw.

The Donkey and the Gardener

The donkey cried out to the king of the gods,
Zeus, about his owner, the Gardener. 'Tight sod's

'Not feeding me enough. Grant me a change of master.'
So he was transferred to a potter. 'This is a disaster,

'The unbearably heavy loads of fired clay. No way.'
So he passes to a tanner. 'I have to say

'I'm worried he'll tire of me and turn me to leather.
I regret leaving the gardener, altogether.

'I should have listened to the badger, Freddie:
"Why change? Aren't things bad enough already?!"'

The Donkey in the Lion's Skin

The funniest thing I ever saw
Was a donkey doing a lion roar.

The donkey had found a lion skin
And wriggled and struggled to put it on.

Then he ran all over the place
Scaring all the silly beasts. What a disgrace!

But in the end he met with the fox
Who listens closely to the voice, and clocks

Something not quite right. He's no fool.
'I hear your bray. You're a donkey or a mule.'

And so the donkey was revealed
As a fraud, by the fox, in the middle of the field.

The Panther and the Goat

You remember the tale of the wolf and the lamb?
Well this is similar. I am

Ready to relate or rather float
The related story of The Panther and the Goat.

'Well, get on with it' I hear you cry.
'Patience young ones', say I , say I.

There was a goat on a mountain slope
Strayed into the path of a panther. Like a dope.

Everyone knew this was the panther's haunt.
Her eyes were bright and her haunches gaunt.

Her black fur shone like new.
There was nothing the goat could do.

'You trod on my tail', the panther said.
'I was trying to get some shut-eye'. Dead

Were her eyes although they were bright.
Dead were her eyes, a fearful sight –

'I didn't mean to, Madam Panther'
Said the goat. He thought a polite answer

Might help, even though he didn't do
What she accused him of. 'And you

'Have scared off all my prey.
Look, they've all run away.'

'It's certainly rather quiet round here'
He replied, as in the distance one sole deer

Clattered across a bit of scree, and off
Into the woods beyond. The panther began to scoff:

'I wonder how you can repay
For all the game you drove away?

'Any idea?' And she looked him up and down.
Then the goat knew he would never get to town.

The Travellers and the Bear

Two mates on a walking tour,
Friends from long before.

Rucksacks, cagouls, tents.
You know the scene. No expense

Spared. Neatly trimmed beards. Shades.
Would look at home in the everglades.

Anyway, there they were,
In the middle of sunny Canada

Or was it the wilds of Greece or Spain?
There they were, two friends again

Not having met for years.
Good times. Hard walking. A few beers.

You know the sort of scene.
Without being mean

They were friends, but their friendship
Wasn't tested. Not yet. Flip

A coin to see which one cares more
For the other. Neither wore

Their heart on their sleeve.
You wouldn't believe

What civilised society can hide.
But let's return. Walk by their side.

The heat and heaviness of the air
And all their hard endeavour

Is making them sweat.
They have a strong scent, don't forget.

It's getting later in the day
And they decide to make camp beside a lone tree.

Good view out across the valley.

[78]

Backpacks off they just lay

Legs tired, summoning the will
To do all the stuff that still

Needed to be done.
Then suddenly, the fun

Was over. At about a hundred yards
A bear, not looking like he wanted to play cards.

Big, brown, how was it that he could
Manage to look both cuddly and real bad?

Moved fast towards them. No sooner had
This happened than one had

Scarpered up the tree
Climbing quickly

As though his friend,
Who thought this was the end,

Didn't exist.
Honest.

The lad who's left decides to play dead,
And just lies there terrified.

He's heard somewhere that a bear
Won't touch a corpse. He hopes. Not a hair

On his head moves, as the beast arrives
And rifles through their things. Dives

Into rucksacks, rips, then comes and sniffs
All over the boy. He coughs

A bear cough, deep and resonant.
Then just moves off with a pleasant

Lollop to his gait.
The lads wait and wait.

Eventually
The one up the tree

Comes down. 'What did he say?
What did the bear whisper in your ear

'When I was stuck up there?'
'Some very good advice, Ray.

'He said "A friend is not a friend
Who deserts you when you need a hand".'

Aesop and the Ferryman

Fella called Aesop. Ever heard of him?
They used to say the story went like this:
One day he made a crossing on a whim.

You know, a change of scene, feel the wind kiss
Your face, watch the sea's ever changing
Ripple, wave, white horses surface.

Apart from anything and everything
Else, in the hope to re-start and refresh
His imagination. Nicely deranging,

Sometimes, a sea trip can be, if you're not neche.
Anyway he paid the man and climbed aboard.
'I remember you', the ferryman says, 'Sess-

'-ion in Athens a while back with your mate ... Claud?
Well I never did. Still writing little stories?
Some kind of job. People not yet got bored?'

'Tales are one of life's eternal glories'
Aesop found himself replying in defence.
'Odysseus, the whirlpool Charybdis, the Furies'

'But you write about hens and frogs and shit like that. Dense.'
'Well, all I can say, boatman, is that my job
May be somewhat more secure than yours. For instance,

'I mentioned Charybdis. They say her great gob
Has already taken two enormous gulps of sea.
The first revealed the mountains. The second made islands bob

'Into view. The third, so the wisest people say,
Will completely drain the oceans altogether.
What will you do then with this old ferry?!'

That shut the ferryman up. He didn't bother
Trying to answer. He just put on a merry
Face, and concentrated his eyes to weather.

The Cat, Mice, Rat and Hen

A cat, a big fat storehouse cat
Who has fed for years on mouse and rat
Lately has discovered that

They're wise to him.
He's not exactly slim.
Not exactly one of the seraphim.

So he needs a new device
To kill the ones who steal the rice.
There's no use being nice.

He'll be out of a job
If he lets them rob
Any more rice or corn on the cob.

So he makes a plan.
He hangs like a sack from the ceiling. Man,
He was desperate. Certain

Death if he was thrown out.
So he hangs there. Nowt
In his mind, within, without,

Proper Zen.
Just then
Another hen,

A rat, three mice
All toshed out nice
Saunter into the place.

'I think I'll have the corn'
Said the rat, all forlorn.
'Me too' said the hen. 'No quorn?'

Said the mice together.
Then soft as a feather
The cat dropped down. Hell for leather

They ran, but he caught
And killed every one. Fought
Like a tiger. Bought

Himself more time
In the job. Went home.
Washed off the grime.

The Fowler and the Blackbird

'What are you doing?' said the blackbird,
Seeing a fowler bending his net.
'Laying foundations. Don't say a word.
For a City none will forget.'

The blackbird waited until he'd gone,
Then flew to the bait in the net.
And, in my opinion,
There isn't a city there yet.

The Cockerel and the Jewel

A cockerel pecking at a dung hill finds
An incredibly precious jewel.
Enough to buy a horse or a mule.
More, in fact, all sorts, all kinds

Of things. But the cockerel's looking for corn.
'What use have I for such as you?'
He says to the sapphire sitting in the poo,
And he wanders off in scorn.

The Bird in Borrowed Feathers

'Jackdaw, Jackdaw, what are those strange feathers for?'
And the peacock and all the birds grabbed back
The plumes he'd stolen a while before.

It nearly gave him a heart attack.
They stripped and stripped, even removed
His own feathers, grey and black.

Until he was a sorry sight. Which proved
That to adorn oneself in borrowed plumes is more
Risky than he'd previously assumed.

The Crow and the Sheep

'Don't perch on my back like that'
Said the sheep to the crow.
'If you did it to a dog, you'd soon know.'

'Despise the weak. Yield to the strong. That
Is my motto.
You, with your cotton

'Wool coat, I can bully rotten.
Dogs, lions, eagles I must flatter.'
'Morality doesn't matter?'

Asked the sheep, sheepishly.
'I pay it lip service. Occasionally.
Only when I have to.'

Said the crow.
Regally.
And off he flew.

The Eagle and the Archer

'I am undone', croaked the eagle,
With an arrow through its heart.
'You've used my feathers for your dart.
Mr Archer, is that legal?'

The Frog and the Ox

Friends call him Mr Competitive.
And sure enough, when the frog sees the ox
He inflates and inflates, very repetitive,
But compelling as one of those Tik-Toks.

He grows and he grows,
He blows and he blows.
Then explodes all over the fox.

The Woman and the Fish

A woman played an oboe
To make the fish dance.
Funny thing. The oboe was pink.
The fish refused. 'No chance'
Said one. 'Oh no'
Said another. Quite a stink
It caused down at her club.

The next day she brought a net,
Lifted them out, and watched them fret.
'Why, you'll dance for me now, all right', she tried to rub

It in. 'It's just that we're celebrating'
Said the fish, even though they were dying,
'Celebrating you've stopped making that awful racket.'

The Deer Without a Heart

'The lion is gravely ill'
Said the fox to the deer.
'You should visit him. His will ...
From what I hear ...'

So the deer went off
To find his den.
The lion bit off
Her ears. 'Never again'

Said the deer to the fox.
'Just a rough caress.
Life's full of hard knocks.
The lion's dying. Bless.'

Some time went by
Then the fox again
Persuaded the deer by
Mentioning the lion's will. 'Ten

Million he's worth, I hear.'
And eventually the deer
Went off once more
Where she went before.

This time the lion killed her.
A medicine man had told him
'Eat the ears and heart of a deer
And you'll recover.' Slim

Sly fox meanwhile snook by
And nabbed the heart from the hart's corpse,

[87]

And when questioned by the lion why
This deer lacked a heart, he smacks his chops

Saying 'The deer was a fool
To visit a lion in its lair.
And since the intellect, as a rule,
Is located there,

The deer can't have had one,
Don't you think?'
And he looked at the lion,
His mouth stained red, like ink.

Printed in Great Britain
by Amazon